Pressing In!
A Woman's Stand

By Marilyn Braxton
Preface and Afterword
by Dean Braxton

Published in Beaverton, Oregon, by Good Book Publishing.
www.goodbookpublishing.com
V1.1

Printed in the United States of America

Table of Contents

Foreword

Christians are constantly bombarded with the admonition to have "faith" — throughout the Bible, or from a pastor, family, friends or even when we proclaim it to ourselves.

A time comes for us to put our true faith in God to the test when our loved ones are in serious illness, even to the point of death. We don't want bad things to happen, but no one knows tomorrow except for God. We have some control in life at times, but at other times, we don't.

As Christians, we need to have faith when we are faced with challenges because Jesus Christ has won the victory. In Him, we are fulfilled; therefore, we can put faith to work with the Word of God and go to it with a focused passion.

This is what my sister, Marilyn, had to do. She combined the Word of God with faith in order to bring healing for her husband, Dean.

She wore the armor of God (Ephesians 6:12-17) and battled the devils with her nonstop prayers, her family and the body of Christ. She had the mindset that she was unstoppable!

The process was not an easy one, but it was a choice Marilyn had settled in her mind to finish! She put the Word of God to work; the Word is Truth. The Word will work if you work along with it.

Pressing In!

Marilyn prayed and proclaimed that Dean was healed. She called "things that were not as though they were" (Romans 4:17). When he received his healing, all she could do was to thank and praise God.

By the way, Marilyn is my prayer partner.

I love you always, sis,
Mi-Sun Haymond

Introduction

I praise and honor God for the favor He has shown the Braxton family.

In the Bible, God gives us accounts of women of great faith. We are blessed to live in the 21st century with women who continue to manifest great faith.

I am blessed to be able to bear witness to such a woman, my daughter-in-law, Marilyn Braxton.

My husband and I flew to Tacoma, Washington, on May 6, 2006. Marilyn put on the full armor of God (Ephesians 6:10-18) during my son's illness and revival from death.

I am so grateful to God for her faith, her obedience to God, her full armor stance and for allowing her to go boldly before the throne in prayer to ask for the healing of her husband, my son, Dean Braxton. On Mother's Day, Sunday, May 14, 2006, my son, Dean, was transferred from Tacoma General Hospital's Intensive Care Unit (ICU) to a sixth-floor room where Marilyn led us in prayer.

I shall always be grateful to God and my daughter-in-law, a woman of strong faith, for the precious gift of another Mother's Day spent with my son here on earth.

All praises to God for using Marilyn as a blessing to our son and the Braxton family.

Pressing In!

As the song goes, "To God be the glory for the things He has done."

Mrs. Freddie Mae Braxton,
Grateful Mother-in-law

Preface
Raising Me from the Dead

By Dean A. Braxton

This book is about a battle my wife had to fight for a life on this earth. She did something that many of us would like to do — help raise someone from the dead with the power of God, someone totally healed today. Me. And for this I am forever grateful.

Medical records validate that my heart stopped for one hour and 45 minutes. Also, my vital organs shut down. But, I not only returned to this earth and lived again, I was totally healed of all physical problems.

The complete story, with the glorious details about how I met Jesus face-to-face and walked among precious loved ones who have died, is told in the book, *In Heaven! Experiencing the Throne of God.*

Pressing In! A Woman's Stand was excerpted from that book to show others how my wife *pressed in* and victoriously claimed God's powerful promises for my life and healing. She covers these 10 keys:

> **Key 1:** *She first reached out to those she believed would stop and pray.*
> **Key 2:** *In the midst of the storm, she praised God.*

Key 3: *She had a close walk with God before this incident had happened.*

Key 4: *She kept her mind on what the Bible said.*

Key 5: *She acted on what she read Paul had done in the Bible.*

Key 6: *She protected her husband from negative people and prayers.*

Key 7: *She was in this battle to win and fought with whatever godly sacrifices it took.*

Key 8: *She took control of her thinking and kept her mind on God's promises.*

Key 9: *She kept pressing in to God and relying on God's strength.*

Key 10: *She knew Whose power and strength was helping her through the difficult moments.*

In this small book, you will read what it took for her to get what she wanted within God's will. She knew that it was not God's will that I die May 5, 2006; she knew God had a plan still for me on this earth that we are currently fulfilling. So as you read on, know that you can have the same result in anything you believe that is within God's will. As you read *Pressing In! A Woman's Stand*, we pray you come to know how the power of God's Word can truly work in this world today.

Marilyn's Testimony

Thursday, May 4

"Mrs. Braxton, please pick up your husband, Dean, from the emergency room and take him home."

Stunned, I clicked off the phone. It was noon. *What in the world is Dean doing in the HOSPITAL?*

"I need to leave," I told the charge nurse, picking up my purse. I was working at another hospital.

When I got to Dean's room, he was asleep from the pain medication they had given him. The emergency room doctor told me that he had kidney stones and a kidney infection with one of the stones located high up on his right side, which was the one that was causing Dean the most pain. The doctor suggested Dean stay overnight for IV antibiotics and fluids. Dean was in and out of the conversation due to the sedation caused by the pain medication.

Later that evening, a urologist (kidney specialist) stopped by to see Dean. He suggested blasting the stones with ultrasound on Friday morning so he would not have to endure more pain. We agreed, knowing he'd be home the next day.

When I left the hospital, Dean was having chills and had a fever, but was sleeping in intervals.

Friday Morning, May 5

Dean was out of it due to the medication with a temperature of 104, but still went into surgery.

While in the surgery waiting area answering questions, Dean asked if the process was over, but he had not even gone into the operating room.

After surgery, Dean was in recovery for almost three hours. I spent the last half hour with him there. While we waited, the doctor who had administered Dean's pain medicine in surgery said Dean had a very bad infection and needed to go to the Intense Care Unit (ICU) to receive fluids, more antibiotics and to be observed. Dean complained that his oxygen mask was uncomfortable, and the nurses changed it for him. He was attached to different IV pumps in his arm.

When we got to the ICU room, I talked to my husband only briefly, when the ICU doctor told us they wanted to put a PICC line (Peripherally Inserted Central Catheter) in Dean's neck so they could take away some of the lines in his arm. This would make it much easier for staff to draw blood for tests. Dean understood, and I left so they could start the procedure.

When I returned to the room after the PICC line had been inserted, I noticed my husband was hardly breathing, and his lips looked ashy. I asked what happened, and the doctor told me they reached a blockage in Dean's neck and that they needed to intubate (put a tube down Dean's throat) or he could die. And there was no time to think about it.

We lived five minutes from the hospital, and I left as they were doing this procedure to pick up some things (of course, praying on the way).

I had barely driven out of the hospital when the surgeon called me on my cell phone to tell me my husband coded (his heart stopped), and they were doing Cardiopulmonary Resuscitation (CPR).

"What?" I couldn't believe it.

I called our son and daughter, Gabriel and Tiffany, who were away at college, to tell them to pray for their dad. I continued home, praying more intensely and calling others, asking them to pray, also. I called a friend who was on her way to the hospital, and she said she would come by to pick me up.

When we arrived at the hospital, we did not see Dean right away, for they were still trying to save his life. I immediately called his parents. They had been visiting relatives in Texas and had to return to California. They talked with the doctor and promised to get to Washington to see their son as fast as they could.

The doctors worked on Dean for an hour and 45 minutes. During this time, friends showed up, and we prayed together in the waiting area in faith for his life. After we prayed, I felt compelled to sing a song of praise and glorify the Lord.

Key 1:
Marilyn reached out to those she believed would stop and pray — for Dean, herself and the doctors.

Key 2:
In the midst of the storm, Marilyn praised God. She pressed into Him rather than running away from Him.

The doctor told me things were very touch-and-go and that they would know more by morning. People in many places throughout the world were praying for Dean. We did not demand God in prayer, we did not beg Him, but we asked the Father in Jesus' name. We thanked the Lord God that Dean was healed by the stripes of Jesus. I refused to doubt, but rather trusted the Word of God for His promise concerning Dean's life.

I knew I had access to the throne of grace and that I could go boldly as a child of the Most High. Not only did I ask, but also I thanked the Lord for what He was doing in Dean even though the circumstances looked bad. I purposed in my heart not to blame God, for it is the devil that comes to steal, kill and destroy. Jesus comes to give abundant life, and I claimed that life for my husband.

John 10:10 (NKJV)
The thief does not come except to steal, and to kill, and to destroy. I [Jesus] have come that they may have life, and that they may have it more abundantly.

Key 3:
Marilyn had a close walk with God before this incident. She was reading her Bible and praying on a continual basis. She knew what the Bible said about this situation. She knew that Jesus came to give abundant life, and Satan came to steal, kill and destroy. So she went to battle knowing what

her God came to do. That was to give abundant
life, and at that time, Dean was not living that life.

It was all so crazy. Before I left the hospital, Dean's body was filling up with the fluids they were putting in him. I felt the need to go home and battle the enemy, for I did not know what the rest of the night would bring Dean. A friend, Francine, and her son, Jordan, stayed overnight with me.

Hospital staff told me later that by morning Dean was taking several medications, including insulin. It didn't look good.

When I arrived home, I cried. I thanked the Lord for what a good husband Dean had been (he put up with me). I thanked the Lord that he was such a good father to our children. I released the angels of God to be encamped roundabout Dean. I did not get much sleep that night and found myself on the floor the next morning, as I would do the next three mornings, praying in the spirit. There is power in the shed blood of Jesus, and I covered Dean in that blood.

Saturday Morning, May 6

Normal blood sugar is 100-110/120. Dean's blood sugar was 500. Doctors told me he needed to be transferred to a different hospital, Tacoma General, to be on kidney dialysis continually because his kidneys did not function at all during the night, and his body was going into septic shock. Dean's body was very large from the fluids. He was on 100 percent ventilation (the machine completely breathing for him). Dean traveled by ambulance 10 to 15 miles that day with a nurse to care for the pumps, the breathing tube and to suction him if needed.

I could see that even through this relocation, God was working. Dean's hospital was part of the Franciscan Health System; they could transfer him to one of the other three sister hospitals in the local area, but in this case, they sent him to a hospital outside of their system. This is amazing because I knew some of the nurses and doctors who would be working with Dean at Tacoma General Hospital. When I talked to the supervisor of nurses that was in charge that day, someone I knew because I had worked at this hospital before, she expressed astonishment that Dean was my husband and was very glad that she had chosen to take him at Tacoma General. She said when she got the call that day to take this critically ill patient from St. Francis Hospital, somehow she knew she should take him. The Lord is good!

Dean had a very good nurse on duty that morning at the new hospital. The nurse was very positive, and I knew that we would get along. A nurse hooked Dean up to dialysis right away, and he lay in the bed without a clue what was going on. Many came to pray for him, and many made themselves available to me if I needed anything.

I refused to accept a negative report. I did not deny there were negative reports, I just refused to accept them and refused to let those reports be the final answer.

One doctor told me it could be a long time before Dean recovered, and he could have brain damage. I told him he *could* get well quickly.

Key 4:
Marilyn heard what the doctor said to her and did not argue with him about his diagnosis, but she kept her mind on what the Bible said. The doctors were doing the best they could, but Marilyn knew that Jesus could heal him.

When I got home that night, I prayed for Dean long, hard and loud. I told the devil — who comes to steal, kill and destroy — to take his hands off my husband! My body felt as if it was on fire as sweat dripped onto my nightshirt. It got so wet, I took it off and laid it across a chair in my bathroom. I took the shirt with me the next morning to the hospital and laid it on Dean's head.

Acts 19:11-12 (NKJV)
Now God worked unusual miracles by the hands of Paul, so that even handkerchiefs or aprons were brought from his body to the sick, and the diseases left them and the evil spirits went out of them.

Key 5:
Marilyn acted on what she had read Paul had done in the Bible. She knew the power of God was on

her that night before and wanted that power transferred to me. She had read in the Bible how God's healing power was transferred through clothes and healed.

Tiffany and Gabriel prayed continually and put their dad on a prayer chain with several of their friends in school.

I did not want anything negative spoken over my husband or to him, nor did I want any negative or hopeless prayers prayed. I remember saying to the Father, "I curse every negative word and prayer spoken over or to my husband in the name of Jesus!" I really did not want anyone visiting Dean and feeling sorry for him or thinking that there was no hope. Death and life are in the power of the tongue, and I made sure my tongue spoke life, for THE WORD OF GOD IS LIFE! I did not have time, nor did I make the time, to pity Dean; I was in a battle, and I wanted to win.

Proverbs 18:21 (NKJV)
Death and life are in the power of the tongue, and those who love it will eat its fruit.

Key 6:
Marilyn protected Dean from negative people and prayers.

Key 7:
She was in this battle to win, and whatever godly sacrifices it took, she was going to make them.

Sunday, May 7

We sang praises in the waiting area, and afterward, a friend of ours, Ycaza, preached to us from the Word of God. We would not give up on Dean. My daughter phoned me and told me to read Psalm 40, and when I did, the first verses ran in my heart: "I waited patiently for the Lord: and He inclined to me, and heard my cry." It gave me such a peace and comfort. I relied completely on the Lord, and He heard my cry for help.

My son called every day to talk to the doctor or nurse about his dad's condition. Once, this thought came to my mind: *Get the funeral ready.* Immediately, I brought my thoughts into captivity to the obedience of Christ, and I told the devil he was and is a liar. I continued to thank God for His promise in Psalm 103:3, for forgiving all Dean's iniquities and healing all of his diseases.

Psalm 103:3 (NKJV)
Who forgives all your iniquities, Who heals all your diseases.

GLORY! Dean doesn't remember this, but he *did* respond the same day. He opened his eyes and looked around as if to say, *What is going on?* I told him I loved him, and so did one of his friends with me. The nurse did not want him to get too excited and increased the sedative and put him back to sleep.

Key 8:
Marilyn kept her mind on the Word of God, even when it was not looking good for Dean. She took control of her thinking and kept it on God's promises.

Monday, May 8
Dean's parents arrived. Praise God! For the next few days, my mother-in-law and I sang to Dean, read James 5:13-15 and anointed him with oil.

James 5:13-15 (NKJV)
Is anyone among you suffering? Let him pray. Is anyone cheerful? Let him sing psalms. Is anyone among you sick? Let him call for the elders of the church, and let them pray over him, anointing him with oil in the name of the Lord. And the prayer of faith will save the sick, and the Lord will raise him up. And if he has committed sins, he will be forgiven.

Sometimes Dean's father would go somewhere else to pray.

I was tired in the body, but my spirit was strong. I was so tired one night when I arrived at the house, I turned the car off, put my head back and fell fast asleep. Shivering from the cold, I awoke about an hour or so later and went into the house and prayed.

All this has happened so fast and unexpectedly, I thought. *How could this minor medical problem with kidney stones cause my husband's heart to stop, cause him to be placed on a breathing machine 100 percent, cause a high blood sugar of 400 to 500 and cause him to be placed on kidney dialysis 24 hours a day every day? How could something so* minor *turn out to be so* major*?*

I continued to press in closer to the Lord.

Key 9:
Marilyn kept pressing in to God and relying on God's strength.

Dean's progress was like riding a roller coaster — his temperature would rise, then the tests would come back negative; his white blood count would skyrocket, then he'd get better.

I continued to trust God. Dean was on six different medications; most were for his blood pressure, one very detrimental to his health, the doctors told me.

One of our friends prayed for Dean with such compassion that he kissed Dean's feet as he was praying. He had no idea of the condition my husband's feet were in — underneath those hospital socks, Dean's toes were purple and black from the medicine, and he had lost feeling in them. We found out later the doctors were planning on cutting his toes off because of poor circulation — they were completely without life. But Dean's toes were saved.

Dean also had a feeding tube in for a couple of days toward the end of his stay in ICU.

Tuesday, May 9

By the fifth day, Dean was healing fast. It surprised the doctors and nurses and other staff who knew his case. One doctor would say, "He is getting better, but we still need to take it slow."

Another doctor would say, "Wow, he's improved 200 to 300 percent in such a short time!"

Many things still happened as Dean's body was healing. The nurse was extremely happy when Dean could follow commands and told the doctor the next day that he was still following commands and that Dean had not skipped a beat. The night of May 9, I came home and purposed in my heart that I would spend all night in prayer for Dean and found out the next day that a friend said he was tired of the situation and also prayed that same night, all night.

Wednesday Morning, May 10

Five young boys from high school showed up to pray for Dean during school hours. These boys touched the heart of the nurse that morning, and he said he would never forget their prayers and love, nor the presence he felt in the room.

On this day, Dean was taken off the ventilator and

dialysis. The nurses asked him if he was in any pain, and he shook his head no. They also explained the procedure for removing the breathing tube and that another breathing treatment would have to be given a half hour later to make sure he could stay off the ventilator.

The nurses told my in-laws and me to take a long lunch break. Prior to leaving for lunch, I whispered in Dean's ear, "Breathe for me, breathe for your children and breathe for your friends … BREATHE!" He nodded, with a puzzled look on his face as if to ask, *What happened?* Dean had this look before but was unable to speak because of the tube.

By this time, Dean was down to taking only one to two medications. Praise God! Psalm 68:35 was one of the scriptures I held onto, for I needed God's strength and His power.

Psalm 68:35 (NKJV)
O God, You are more awesome than Your holy places. The God of Israel is He who gives strength and power to His people. Blessed be God!

Key 10:
Marilyn knew whose power and strength was helping her through.

After a great lunch with a friend, I arrived in his room again and found Dean sitting up in bed! It was good to hear his voice again. I, along with many of the nurses who did not have Dean as a patient, celebrated his recovery. The nurses were glad to see someone who had made it through all of this; because it was Nurse's Week, they needed to have a happy ending themselves.

Other staff came by to see the progress Dean had made, calling it a "Miracle" and calling him the "Miracle Man." Boy, did we know that! The fluid was leaving Dean's body, and his kidneys were working fine.

Then Dean asked me the big question: "Would you please sit down and tell me what happened?"

When I told him, he cried, and of course, I told him more than once. He wanted to know every detail. It really touched him to know so many cared and prayed, many that we had never met before and some we have yet to meet.

Then my husband's eyes clouded as he lay in the hospital bed, as though he was suddenly being transported to another place — a beautiful place. His countenance softened as a smile spread across his face. He searched for the words to tell me what was bubbling up inside.

"I have seen Jesus three times, and the first time, He said, *'No, it is not your time. Go back.'*" His eyes flashed with excitement, and I could tell there was more.

"I stared at Jesus' compassionate, deeply loving eyes with awe and wonder. As though to answer my unspoken question, He said to me a second time, *'No, it is not your time. Go back.'*"

The back of my neck tingled as what my husband was

saying to me began to sink in: While I was on my knees praying for his heart to start beating again, Dean was standing *face-to-face* with our Lord and Savior, Jesus!

Dean paused, looked away, up at the ceiling — no, beyond the ceiling — amazed again at the scene he'd witnessed. Then he turned his face back to me with tears brimming in his eyes. "I didn't want to leave this glorious place. But Jesus told me a third time, *'No, it is not your time! Go back!'* He blinked back the tears, melting before me. "Everything is *right* where Jesus is, and there is nothing wrong. I fell to my knees in worship and adoration and cried out, 'You did this for me? *Thank You! Thank You! Thank You!'*"

It was hard for me to imagine that, while Dean's body was lying in ICU as the doctors worked feverishly to revive him, his spirit was in heaven beholding the beautiful face of our Savior.

Dean told me he could have expressed his gratitude for what Jesus had done for him for the next 3,000 years or more and still would have wanted to keep going.

"Jesus is bright, and where Jesus is, everything is *right.* Jesus is brighter than our sun, but we can still look at Him." Dean's face seemed to glow as he shared his incredible experience.

Dean was making a remarkable recovery, here the sixth day after he died for an hour and a half and went to heaven. He could now sit for 15 minutes in a chair.

This was the first night I stayed with him; I was his nurse that night.

May 14, Mother's Day

Doctors moved Dean to another floor. He walked down the long hall to the family visiting room and could not feel his toes. Despite this, doctors were still in awe of the miracle that had taken place before their eyes.

Dean spent 13 days in the hospital, and nine of those days were in ICU.

James 5:16 (NKJV)
The effective, fervent [red-hot] prayer of a righteous man avails much.

We give God Almighty all the glory, for He is faithful to His Word.

May 16 and Beyond

Dean came home and recovered for one and a half months. When he returned to King County Superior Court as the manager of special courts, he worked half days for five weeks.

His toes are completely healed. He is not taking any medications. After five weeks, he returned to working full time.

Dean has had several checkups and tests since he has been home, and the doctors give him a clean bill of health.

One doctor told Dean he should tell the story of the miracle that he is alive.

Another doctor told Dean, "A lot of people prayed hard for you."

One of the critical care doctors, who knew me from when I worked at the hospital, told me candidly, "I was so scared; I have not been that scared in a long time because things happened so fast."

Dean has been back to the hospital to visit, and they are still saying what a miracle it is. They asked him to make rounds with them one day, so that others on staff could see him.

Later, we found out that when the doctor blasted the stones, the poisons from the infection got into his bloodstream, and all of his vital organs shut down. One nurse told us later, "We have bad outcomes with these cases."

Psalm 14:1 (NKJV)
The fool has said in his heart, "There is no God."

Well, there is a God, He is alive and miracles do happen. He is the Great Jehovah, God Almighty, Lord of Lords and King of Kings! I bless the readers of this testimony in Jesus' name. My prayer for you is that you take up your cross and follow Jesus daily and that you walk a life pleasing to Him. And that He becomes the lover of your soul as He is mine, in Jesus' name.

A Summary of Marilyn's 10 Keys for Pressing In

Key 1: *Marilyn first reached out to those she believed would stop and pray.*

Key 2: *In the midst of the storm, she praised God.*

Key 3: *She had a close walk with God before this incident had happened.*

Key 4: *She kept her mind on what the Bible said.*

Key 5: *She acted on what she had read Paul had done in the Bible.*

Key 6: *She protected her husband from negative people and prayers.*

Key 7: *She was in this battle to win and whatever godly sacrifices it took.*

Key 8: *She took control of her thinking and kept it on God's promises.*

Key 9: *She kept pressing in to God and relying on God's strength.*

Key 10: *She knew Whose power and strength was helping her through.*

Pressing In!

I am living proof that these keys work because God brought me back to life by the power of His Word and my faithful wife's prayers.

Many Blessings,
Dean A. Braxton

Pressing In

By Dorothea Holmes

The Devil is a liar
He is not your friend
When he knocks at your door
Start Pressing In
He hits below the waist
And will fight you to the end
It's an attack on your faith
Start Pressing In
He comes to kill, steal and destroy
Fighting you tooth and nail
Stand firmly on the Word
Start Pressing in
Go boldly to the throne
Making your request known
Putting on the full armor of God
Start Pressing In
Breastplate of righteousness
The shield of faith
Helmet of salvation
Sword of the Spirit
And your feet shod with the preparation
Of the Gospel of Peace
Dress from Head to toe

Pressing In!

You won't bend, bow or break
The righteous always prevail
Make no mistake
The devil doesn't quit
He will knock again
Pretending to be your friend
Stand firm and believe God's Word
Remember the promises He made to you
Where you Press In
He Presses With You

Afterword

By Dean Braxton

Medical Records and Transcripts

Before this incident took place, I was a very healthy 47-year-old male. I had regular physical checkups, mostly because I was in the United States Air Force on active duty for six years and reserve duty for 14 years. I retired from the Reserves with a clean bill of health. The only problem I had after that was kidney stones in June 2002, four years prior to this incident.

I went through the same procedure back then for kidney stones as I did for this incident. The biggest difference was staying in the hospital overnight before the operation. During the first incident, I checked into the hospital that morning and came out in the afternoon of the same day.

The following is taken from the medical records we received from both hospitals where I stayed. Now, to get these records was not easy because of the mistakes that were made and the potential of a lawsuit. The doctor who made the mistakes made it hard for us to receive accurate reports. Finally, we had to get other doctors who worked on my case to give us the information.

Pressing In!

It has never been our intention to sue the doctor or the hospital. We just wanted the official medical records to support the medical testimonies we had received from doctors, nurses and other people who worked in the hospitals.

It has also been hard to get a medical professional to read the records and write it down for this book. We came up against resistance from people not wanting to go on record in translating the medical account. They, too, did not want to support in writing the number of mistakes the urologist and hospital made. Again, they did not want to be a part of any potential lawsuit in the future. So, the following is raw information that you will have to translate yourselves.

During the four years after the first treatment for kidney stones, I did not have any problems with kidney stones or any other illness. I do not remember taking any sick leave for personal illness.

After my recovery, I received resistance from the doctor who did not at first want to take out a stint placed in my body. My wife called the doctor and firmly told him she would take legal action if we did not receive an appointment to have the stint removed. The doctor finally consented to see me the next day and removed the stint.

I asked him at that time what happened to cause my heart to stop. He said that I had a bad infection that he thought was taken care of with some very strong medicine. But for some reason, the infection was not affected by that medicine. He said they had not checked prior to the operation if the medicine worked or not and had assumed it did. It was not until five days later that they found out from lab reports that the medicine did not have any effect on the infection.

At the time of the incident, the doctor did not know what was going wrong or why my vital organs were shutting down. The doctor told me that if they had not done everything right, and instead 10 minutes earlier or 10 minutes later, I would have been behind the eight ball (dead).

I also asked him if I had died. He said my heart had stopped and that every time it looked like it was going to start, it would not. He said they worked on me about one hour and 30 minutes (official records state one hour and 45 minutes). I asked him if he saw this as a miracle, and he said it was and that I should go tell the story.

As you can read in the Appendix, there were a lot of things that just went wrong with the procedures and my body. Thank God my wife, Marilyn, *stood on God's Word and promises to her and pressed in!*

Appendix

Excerpts of Information Taken from My Medical Records and Medical Transcripts

Preoperative Diagnosis:
Left ureteral calculus and bilateral nephrolithiasis (kidney stones) and pyelonephritis (urinary tract infection)

Postoperative Diagnosis:
Left ureteral calculus and bilateral nephrolithiasis and pyelonephritis

Operation:
Cystoscopy with retrograde pyelogram, push back of ureteral calculus and bilateral extracorporeal shock wave lithotripsy

Indications:
This delightful 49-year-old gentleman [actually 47] presented to the hospital with pyelonephritis and obstruction ureteral calculus. After 24 hours of antibiotic coverage with supplemental antibiotic administration in operation room, he presents at this time for definitive surgical intervention.

Pressing In!

Findings:
Obstructing calculus in the left ureter is pushed back in the renal pelvis, and a 24-cm 7-french double-J stent is left in place in the ureter and that calculus further targets and both kidneys were fragmented with difficulty.

After 2,400 shocks, the procedure was terminated, and the patient was awakened and returned to the recovery room in satisfactory condition. There were no complications. He tolerated the procedure well.

–From a May 6, 2006 report by the surgeon who performed the original operation.

Appendix

Excerpts Taken from the Rest of the Medical Records and Medical Transcripts

- Larger amount of fluid resuscitation for hypertension
- Poorly responsive
- Move legs to pain
- Very cool digits with cyanotic toes
- Acute renal failure
- Secondary to acute tubular necrosis oliguric
- Profound septic shock
- Prolonged Cardiac Arrest
- CPR one hour and 45 minutes
- Septic shock with urasepisis
- Respiratory failure
- Pulmonary infiltrates
- Edema versus adult respiratory distress syndrome
- Post prolonged CPR
- Post cardiac arrest
- Prolonged resuscitation
- Fulminant sepsis
- Too numerous to count stones in right kidney
- Chest x-rays show the development of diffuse pulmonary edema
- Urine culture sent yesterday is growing greater than 100,000 colonies of E. coli.
- Doctor reports spent a total of one hour and 45 min. total critical care time with the patient, not including procedure

Pressing In!

- Severe sepsis
- Diagnosis of SIRS/Sepsis with hypotension, tachycardia, tachypnea, hypoxemia.
- High risk of disseminated intravascular coagulation.
- Cardiac arrest
- Urasepsis with E.Coli.
- Secondary renal shut down
- Asystable
- Extubated
- Herodynamically stable
- Shock liver
- Shock syndrome
- Hemodynamic stress
- On mechanical ventilation
- Paralytic ileus
- Multi-organ failure
- Critically ill
- Prognosis is poor
- Quniton Cathetar and dialysis treatment (risk & benefits)
- Risk for bleeding complication with ongoing DIC
- Clotting dialysis system given ongoing DIC
- Obstruction urinary stones
- Severely acidotic with a lactic acid as high as 16
- Poorly responsive
- Requiring High Fi0 Moderate to servers patchy air space

Appendix

- Opacities in the lungs bilaterally slightly increased. This is ward son for progression of pneumonia.
- Very unfortunate critically ill patient

For more information,
to see the Braxton's travel schedule,
videos or book them to come to your
church or organization,
go to:
www.BraxtonInternational.org
E-mail: deanmarilynbraxton@msn.com
Phone: 253.579.5656

Pressing In! A Woman's Stand published by
Good Book Publishing
www.goodbookpublishing.com
a division of Good Catch Publishing.

To find out how to publish the inspirational
and evangelical dramatic stories of members in
your church, or read others' stories, go to:
Good Catch Publishing at
www.goodcatchpublishing.com.